Free to Roam

Free to Roam

Poems from a Heathen Mommy

Megan Rahm

Minneapolis–St. Paul

Copyright 2020 by Megan Rahm
All rights reserved. No part of this book may be used or reproduced in any manner without written permission except in the case of brief quotations used in reviews. For more information, contact Freethought House at info@freethoughthouse.com.

Cover & interior design by Robaire Ream

ISBN: 9780988493889

For Karly-

My little girl—
spunky, lively, and bright.
Never turn off
that curious brain.

This book is about my journey as an atheist—from the rural area where I grew up to my present-day life as a mom in Toledo, Ohio USA.

Thanks to my family–my husband who is my partner in everything, my four-year-old daughter who can sing louder than anyone in the grocery store, and my parents who restored my sanity on numerous occasions.

I may not be fond of the rural area where I grew up but I will always have good memories of my family there.

Table of Contents

Part I: Curls and Cornfields
Beautiful Country 1
Thrive 2
In the Back of a Pick-Up 3
Christian Admirer 4
When Dreams Come True 5
Unbound Future 6
No Apologies 7
Education 8
Mistreated 9
My Scars, My Story 11
Forbidden 12
Safe 13
I'm Not Really a Joiner 14
I Found Freedom in the City Downriver. 15

Part II: Why I Hate Sunday Morning
Baptism 19
How do you sleep? 20
A Godless Ghazal 21
They Turn Their Backs 22
Grounded 23
A Message for My Daughter 24
Hate 25
The Army in the Distance 26
This is What You Sound Like 27
Stuck in a Closet 28
Truth 29
Summer Storm 30
No Public Displays of Atheism 31
Christianity ≠ Morality 32
Yet 34
Seven Reasons I Don't Speak Up 35
You Call Yourself a Christian 36
Self Pleasure 37
Spread Your Word 38
You Didn't Need God 39
One Day 40
One Absurd Book vs. Facts 41
Crumble 42

Part III: The Nice Heathen Family Next Door

Play Date 45
The Curls 46
Midwest Mom 47
Am I Holding It Together? 48
The Curiosity of a Three-Year-Old 49
Uninvited 50
Growing Pains 51
Hiding in the Bathroom 52
43613 54
Dark Clouds Over Toledo 55
Weekend Aftermath 56
A Little Cheer with Our Cheerios 57
Anxiety 58
The Things We Love 59
Alphabet Soup 60
Family Image 61
Twinkle 63
Dance for Strangers 64
Sleep Lightly 65
She Came in a Storm 66
Non-traditional Student 67
Why Aren't There More Bright Stars? 68

Part IV: Midwest Mom: Meatloaf and Revolution

In the Quiet of the Snow 71
A New War 72
Lead Like a Girl 73
Jump 74
One More 75
I Cleaned My Plate 76
More of Us 77
We'll Keep You Well 78
Anger 79
Our Rope 80
Rise 81
Free to Roam 82
A Mom with Dreams 83
The Path 84
Girl Mom 85
Grit 86

The Virus 88

Part I

Curls and Cornfields

Once a scared little girl
from god's country,
waiting and hidden in a dusty corner,
was hungry for the outside world.

Her day has come.

Beautiful Country

I miss the nights
when lightning bugs speckled the endless horizon
and my eyes bathed in the indigo sky.

My favorite color has always been
newly sprouted winter wheat—
an affirmation of new beginnings.

I loved waking up after a snowstorm
blinding white
and alone in the silence of the barren landscape.

From the delicate irises of spring
to the golden blazes of September
every bug in Henry County fluttered its way into our
 little house.

Dark nights of thunder and wind
made my heart pound to pieces
and sparked a fascination with the dangers of
 the heartland.

Growing up in the country
was a crimson struggle of wits and tears
but I will always cherish the beauty of my childhood
 home.

Thrive
(a message to my younger self)

Thrive
among the stares
meant to strip your future naked.

Thrive
among the words
meant to leave your outlook tainted.

Thrive
outside the conformity
of the minds no longer free.

Thrive
free of the Book
that binds their hands and knees.

Thrive
in your community
on the outside looking in.

Thrive
among your neighbors
ignoring their own sin.

Thrive
because you're strong
and love will always win.

In the Back of a Pick-Up

Brittle bones chilled
beneath frost moon eyes—
she clings to the bed of a truck.
Sticky pebbles clatter off the hungry tires.
Pink sunset flickers
through the singing leaves above.
Rough road ahead.
Alfalfa fields quickly pass by—
purple and green smear across the horizon.
She tightens her grip
as her insecurities whip in the wind.
She's been imprisoned by a home with the biggest sky
but barely a pinprick on the map.
One day despair will grow wings
and a sheltered childhood will be fuel for her
    adventures.
She shivers in the cold
and never looks back.

Christian Admirer

Eyes of lust and honeydew
don't mean I grant you permission
to invade my liberated world.
Drop the slate
and let the luster fade.
If you want in my life
I'm gonna need you raw, be real.
Give up
because you'll never change me.
Your envy shines like emeralds.
I bet purity burns like hell.

When Dreams Come True

When a small town becomes a cage
you fantasize about the future—
a childhood filled with dreams.

One day I'll go to college and absorb everything.
One day I'll have a successful career.
One day I'll have a daughter who looks up to me.

Growing up is painful.
I wish I could go back in time
and tell that little girl her dreams will come true.

You didn't have to go far.
The potential was always in you
and you'll call that city down the river

home.

Unbound Future

Curls burn
leaving risks in my footsteps.
Three cheers for my unpolished stance—
I've gone mudding in my ancestor's field.
It's a dusty outward existence—
no cable
no wings
no choice.
My curls hit the earth
on crumpled daily news.
They blanket my reach with fear of public failure.
Dip a toe in the salty future
because tardy acts trail in the brake lights.
Smile
with eyes that hydrate
and nervous giggles that collect in the drain.

No Apologies

Grinning scarlet and steel—
she approached with a warm amber gaze in her eyes.
His touch left her sailing on the turquoise ocean,
the salty sea breeze in her disheveled hair.
One night of fun under the delicious moonlight—
maybe she'll see him again sometime
or maybe she'll just cherish this memory.

Education
(to the next generation)

Education
breaks past the barriers
presented in my small town,
takes me farther
than the view from the steeple.

Education
is the light
leading me to a future
not promised here.

Education
is my ticket out—
a chance in the outside world,
my escape.

Education
is a way to release their holy grasp.
Around here,
going to public school
doesn't mean you escape indoctrination.

Education
is hope for the generation after me.
I want you to know
high school eventually ends
and you are free to go.

The last school bell rings of sweet freedom.
You are in charge of the rest of your life.

Mistreated

Beads of envy line your forehead—
in your sick game,
you brought fire to the fight.
My impressionable spirit whets your appetite for
    attention.

Peck away at my frazzled brain.
My secret thoughts run down your chin.
Sour doubt and anxiety
appease your fickle cravings.

You could be anywhere—
watching, waiting, stewing in your misery.
Nowhere is safe.
You assert your crumbling power with fear.

A captive victim of your abuse—
your overbite stabs at my fragile existence.
You'll never know the cost of your actions—
a price I'll pay for the rest of my days

I want vengeance
but I want freedom even more.
You're gone but still very much present
in my broken brain.

Thoughts of progress are fleeting,
pain erodes hope.
Your suffocating grip lingers.
I'm shackled from my next chapter.

over →

The cold shadow of trauma
blankets my world.
Maybe with time
healing light will creep back in.

My Scars, My Story

My curls screamed
as they were straightened.
My songs
were stripped from my lungs.
Fresh freedom
was depleted when I gasped.
Shackles of indoctrination
imprisoned my peers.
I was alone.
Time was never on my side
in that small tired town.
Even when I left,
cruel judgment branded
a lasting impression—
scars that are just
a part of my story
that I'll finish in my own words.

Forbidden

I'm drowning in your choppy sea of innocence.
You're ass-deep in constricting dogma.

If you got your chance,
what would you do to me?

Green eyes and icy fingertips stripping me naked,
a bite that burns with intention.

Would you pin me down out of years of frustration
or newfound emancipation? We'll never know.

This secret fantasy only plays out in your head
because god is always watching.

Sweet dreams, farm boy.
I'm going home to wash your shame off my dress.

Safe

Pounding the pavement
on a path lined with righteous onlookers—
my thin skin burns from their judgment.

A community spreading hate
but even more fear
to young minds that know no different.

My family didn't send those same messages.
My brain remained injured in the community
but very much alive with the support of my family.

After a day of drowning in His Word,
I can come home and feel safe
and accepted in my now healing skin.

My parents were the role models
that made me into the woman and mother
I am today.

I'm Not Really a Joiner

I never wanted to be on the outside looking in.
As a child, I wanted to be one of them.
Conformity comes with a community—
acceptance, but only to your face.
Still, I just wanted to belong.

My friends went to church so I joined them.
My skepticism secretly never died.
If I go to church enough, something will click.
I will see what they see.
I can force myself to believe.

In the end, common sense won
and I remained a skeptic.
A somewhat painful memory
became a time that later defined me.

I wish the confidence I feel as an adult
could have helped me through my childhood struggles
but it never works out that way.
Feeling grounded in atheism is a cornerstone
    of strength.

I Found Freedom in the City Downriver

An endless vista of harvest gold and sapphire sky—
why does this beautiful land
come with such a harsh reality?

We all had a role to play.
The cold steeples were watchtowers—
attentive eyes on those who strayed.

The only path to freedom was to leave.
A community hidden from the outside world
but only a forty-minute drive from where I now
    call home.

Part II

Why I Hate Sunday Morning

> The world is an amazing place.
> I see good in my everyday life
> and potential is around every corner.
>
> I don't need god to feel inspired.

Baptism

Every innocent baby
is born tainted
new to the world
but on a direct path to Hell.

A cold splash of submission
followed by pictures and cake
saves their blank slate souls
and fulfills a family's societal duty.

The child has been marked
for indoctrination, brainwashing,
and conformity—
a fresh young mind donning chains and shackles.

Water should just be water
in a meaningless ceremony
but it becomes a deadly weapon
recruiting for a dangerous army.

Let the well dry up
Let the children go free
Let's defeat the army
that has imprisoned us all.

How do you sleep?

Indigo rain cleansing my brain
after a restless night of "soul searching."
Relief comes when you realize god isn't real
and you're released from your rusty chains.

An outlook of debilitating winter
melts and sizzles into freedom.
Like fresh linen under the morning sun—
I put my heart out on the line and won.

I'm the shy queen of my ruby paradise
which resides right here on earth.
I no longer yearn for a flimsy mystery in the clouds.
Breathe deep into the truth and sleep peacefully.

A Godless Ghazal

Growing up in the heavy shadows of your saintly
　façade,
it's lonely in the heartland without God.

With a frightened closet case of godlessness,
I unearthed an inner righteousness without god.

Tears of hot anger bled down my face
grounding me in a clarity only found without god.

My tiny voice shakes your glass kingdom.
The throne shatters with pebbles cast without god.

No longer in the confining shadows, I proclaim
　empathy and love conquer
in a liberated life without god.

My daughter explores with full moon eyes and a
　burning mind.
Curiosity pumps the blood surging through her
　childhood without god.

I treasure life because there's nothing after it.
Launch your embattled skyrocket for this short life
　without god.

They Turn Their Backs

Tall tales grow
from a book of weathered fables.

Long shadows fade
when we look past its hateful pages.

Believers know shame—
they turn their backs on love and freedom.

When His Word dies,
peace will settle on our minds.

Grounded

Ivory giggles and pink powder secrets
power an endless charade.
Let it all hang out
between the pews.
Just once
let the cold stares
see your delicate pearl.
Let lace and tumbleweed
caress your bare skin.
Let your fellow parishioners
blush with envy.
Let reality swallow you whole,
and you'll realize
you don't need to look to the skies—
satisfaction is found right here on the ground.

A Message for My Daughter

A righteous grown-up wrote His Word
on the wall with a Crayola marker.
Bright red.
Out of place.
If I scrub hard enough,
the lies will come off.
The poisonous ink transferred
to the washrag.
My hands are soiled
my fingers ache
my grip weakens.
It's hard work removing stubborn stains from fresh
    minds.
The pain will be worth it.
I soak the rag
in love, empathy, and common sense—
red letters don't stand a chance.
I long for clean walls
for my daughter,
colorful markers now in her tiny hands.

Hate

Can you hate those who hate?
Does that make me just like them?
Can I hate them as much
as they recklessly dish it out?

Gay?
Trans?
Short skirt?
Tarot deck?
Not in their "good" book.

My hate for them
is well-deserved.
It's grounded in observation.
It's revenge for those who are bullied
by that asshole in the sky.

My mouth was bound tight
choking on their fairy tales.
I cut the rope
The shackles
The silence
Their power.

But in the end,
I will treat them with empathy—
because that's what good humans do.
That's something they don't understand.

Hate may be on my mind
but not in my ability.

"Hate the belief but not the believer."
(Isn't that what they say?)

The Army in the Distance

A polished alabaster army
preaches to excess.
I see their reflection in the gunmetal—
another dream dead among the thistles.
They're in prison, too.
The walls are their own—
rusted and sunburnt
so rigid they are fragile.
Their steeple of quicksilver
poisons authentic human touch.
I relish my freedom from a distance
at midnight under the frost.

This is What You Sound Like

Unicorns prance
through chocolate ice cream fields
while singing treasured polkas.

They lick the citrus sky
as purple ribbons rain down.
It was a banana pudding kind of flood.

Everyone believes it so I do, too.
I even have a book that says it's true.
I'm from a good unicorn family.

You don't believe me?
You have no proof that unicorns don't exist.
Prove me wrong. (Not that it will matter.)

Stuck in the Closet

There are crowds of atheists
cloaked in the long shadows of steeples—
even more than we know.

They swallow the truth
because they think they have to,
because maybe they were raised that way.

One, two, ten years
in a dark closet—
their thoughts echo in the loneliness.

They secretly question as
a tortured mind now liberated
yet another voice suppressed.

They're scared
but even more angry.
I know that innermost turmoil.

That anger will fuel progress—
a passionate fire that lights the way.
The most liberated life is an honest one.

Truth

Evidence is everything.
Show me proof
and I'll change my mind.
Question those with influence
and bring their power to our level.
I plant two feet on earth
and let common sense lead the way.
I lick my fingers
after handling the truth.

Summer Storm

My glasses sprouted wings
and lifted my brain to the clouds.
Fat drops of curiosity rained down
flooding the path to heaven.
His Word washed away
in a summer storm.
The sun's rays breakthrough
and pierce my brain—
my inner thoughts exposed.
The burning truth fills in the holes
building a path to peace and love.
My glasses return and perch on my nose.
I see a new humanity.
My brain now rests in a head held high.
The promise of heaven
has stunted growth on earth.
Freedom came in a summer storm
that nourished us all.

No Public Displays of Atheism

You wear a cross on your necklace
cold and shiny,
close to you
for everyone to see.
Your beliefs lead you
define you
publicly.

You assume I'm like you
but I'm not.
I keep my thoughts to myself
fearing ridicule
and discrimination.
My views aren't on display
but I'm proud of who I am—

just sick of hiding in the shadows.

Christianity ≠ Morality

A "god-fearing" man, a "good church-going" woman—somehow "Christian" is synonymous with "moral" and "trustworthy".

That overflowing collection plate meant to do god's work is lining your pastor's pockets as you pray in a church that doesn't pay taxes.

That obnoxious auto mechanic that spent ten long minutes telling me that he's from a "good Christian family" just ripped me off.

That predatory priest just found another young victim—a sick act that will haunt the child for the rest of his life.

That church lady in pearls just called that young girl a slut not knowing of her turbulent life and powerful inner strength. The fight for survival is a daily battle.

That family secret swept under the rug—got to keep up that good Christian appearance as children are silenced once again. Godly children are better seen, not heard.

God's country is stagnant—much-needed progress has stalled again. The inevitable catch up will take decades.

Women are servants, baby factories, and second-class citizens. Her naked body is tightly chained to the cold steeple. No future. No say.

You hate what's different. Be like you or burn in Hell for eternity.

Millions are trapped in their closet that you nailed shut, but our tired brains and hearts are victoriously resilient and bust down the door.

Religion is not required for morality. In fact, it's best that you take it out of the equation altogether.

Yet

I believe there are things we cannot explain.
Yet.
That doesn't mean we should make up answers
rooted in the supernatural.
Sit with and accept
your fear of the unknown.
Science will catch up.

Seven Reasons I Don't Speak Up

1. to avoid confrontation
2. so I don't have to explain myself
3. because we still have to work together and I don't want it to be awkward
4. to avoid discrimination
5. so I can survive Thanksgiving dinner
6. because you won't take me seriously
7. because I was told not to

You Call Yourself a Christian

It's a front
nothing more than an image
an expectation—
not to be taken in a literal sense.

You're indifferent—
a "good" person
from a "good" family.
Christian is merely your label.

How do you really feel?
Are you scared to question?
Are you scared to admit you question?
Are you just too lazy to question?

Your passivity
causes others to suffer.
Saying nothing lets hatred win
and keeps freedom out of reach.

Self-Pleasure

My devilish smile meets your starving eyes
with the intention of sin and fun.

Let me tell you a secret.
Squirm in the pew
and button up your Sunday best
because I'm not going to deny
the natural things my body wants.

Behind closed doors
I'm not afraid to take matters
into my own eager hands.
I hope Jesus is watching
because I've reached a point of no return.

Thick thighs, soft skin,
and toes that curl—
I love being a woman.
I want to honor my beautiful curves
with a release of self-love.

Frank admissions of a healthy act—
your discomfort amuses me.
Fire and an eternity of agony
scare you into faithful submission,
but I burn in your envious eyes.

Do you repent for the things you do
when you're all alone?
Lose your shame, inhibitions, and clothes
and enjoy yourself.
Aren't our bodies amazing?

Spread Your Word

Your newest charity project—
that's how you see me.

Telling me about your god
will make your heart full
and your ego big.

One more point scored
for an eternal life with Jesus.

There's so much love to go around
as long as everyone is just like you.
If not, they'll burn in Hell
your god doesn't love—
He divides.

And you're absolutely right—
I just haven't found the right church yet.
It's a glass slipper that doesn't exist.

"Do unto others"
is a teaching from that holy book
you've probably never read.

I don't need your charity
but I deserve your respect.

You Didn't Need God

You said you couldn't do it alone
but you did.
We are all powerful
in our own lives.
Scale that jagged cliff,
surf those tempest-swept waters—
you are in charge.
You are secretly surefooted,
resourceful with undiscovered confidence.
What you think is strength in god
is really strength within yourself.
You are more capable than you know.

One Day

The roses are overripe under the blood-red sunset.
A harvest of hungry soldiers
feed on stories that never happened.

Their bloated guts ingest the last little sliver of light.
They would feast their eyes on the truth
if they weren't already blinded by empty promises.

Legislation is their deadly weapon of choice
and my liberated existence is caught in the crosshairs.
I scream for help but my morning blue voice is
    silenced.

One day the army will just be ghosts in the smoke
and I will let my titanium guard down
no longer needing to shield myself from their made-up
    world.

One day.

One Absurd Book vs. Facts

How can one outdated book
of lies
hate
fables
and fairytales
hold so much power?
People deny facts.
They argue against science,
believe without evidence

Forget the book.
Would they behave this way in any other context?

Can your mail carrier walk on water?
Did your dentist turn water into wine?

Of course not. That's absurd.

That one book holds their minds captive.
Cherish the book or burn it—
it doesn't matter.
Facts are facts.
They're true whether they believe them or not.

But if they possessed common sense,
life would be a whole lot easier for all of us.

Crumble

People weren't meant to be in flocks
with a one-size-fits-most destiny.

The Bible's pages are thin but not transparent.
His promises crumble like ash.

A future of regrets is blanched and bittersweet.
His Word poisons us all yet the canary continues
   to sing.

Part III

The Nice Heathen Family Next Door

The flickering glow of the streetlights
illuminates opportunities of tomorrow.
In this welded city of midnight and moonstone,
the morning shall greet us all the same.

Play Date

In a quiet neighborhood
tucked between accountability and appearances
I live among you—the outwardly faithful

with my soccer mom SUV,
weekly gymnastics classes,
over-the-top birthday parties,

picky eater battles,
car seat wrestling,
and inevitable grocery store meltdowns.

My silent anger presses
behind my warm, neighborly smile.
Your small talk is carefree and careless.

Would you let your bratty kid
play with my bratty kid
if you knew I was an atheist?

The Curls

The curls grew longer
thicker
escaping in the wind.
She whispers to the dog next door,
"I'll be back tomorrow".
She likes her pizza
sunny side up,
her smile
to brighten the galaxy.
Those curls never go far
because they are a part
of something radiant—
a little girl
with the future under her feet.
She'll walk a mile
then sprint the rest
curls tied tight to her skull.

Midwest Mom

Passive-aggressive with a nervous giggle—
I'm a casserole of sweet and salty.
My soft meat-and-potatoes pudge
keeps me warm in the snow.

I'm a Midwest mom
from a family caught between the farm and the city.
My daughter's urban upbringing
looks a lot different from my childhood in the country.

Generations of strong women before me
have given me a lot to live up to.
We're steeped in tradition
but must keep moving forward.

My little girl's smile lights the way
reaffirming growth in the blackest of swamps.
Tomorrow looks bright if you squint a little.

Am I Holding It Together?

Am I holding it together
just enough?
My little girl,
new to the world—
am I showing her
what she needs to see?
Does each fragile moment,
every breakdown,
every tear count?
Or should I look
at the bigger picture—
her impending future?
Is this struggle
a drop in the bucket
or the straw
that breaks the camel's back?
What matters
is what she sees
through her eyes—
not mine.
She paves her own way.
I merely provide
the asphalt.

The Curiosity of a Three-Year-Old

She arrives perched atop my hip—
messy cheeks and unbound giggles.
Ten little fingers
stretch to the storm,
squeezing the clouds tight.
She sings as cool rain
trickles down her arms.
She cautiously tastes the rising sun.
Burning nectar coats her throat.
In one big gulp,
she swallows the prickly truth.
Her imagination blossoms
into a timid bluebird
soaring above the bay.
The shoreline dissolves into uncertainty—
nowhere to land.
She learns to fly even higher, faster.
Relish the chilling freedom
and feel grounded in your mother's eyes.

Uninvited

Play the part.
Be the picture of politeness.
I'm faking a role,
but so are you.
Loneliness is loud,
but isolation is deafening.
Save face.
The true me is uninvited.

Growing Pains

Untamed exploration
churns up burning questions-to-be.
Her stubby little hands
tightly grip the rotting planet.
They absorb freely flowing ambitions
as particles of future discoveries
spill through her wide-open pores.
Her organic curiosity
roots itself in soft, forgiving soil.
Soak up blood, sweat,
and available knowledge.
Innocence tastes bitter as the long days pass.
Torrential tears
fueled by freshly scraped-up palms
topple the welcome basket.
I bear witness
to her beautiful growing pains.

Hiding in the Bathroom

An afternoon unraveling in tears and rage—
I've reached my limit.

My sanity is in a fragile state
and screaming to be restored.

Whether nature calls or not,
I'm hiding in the bathroom.

The demands of a preschooler
have set my sight on fire.

My waterproof mascara works overtime
as I struggle to keep my head above water.

Mommy's broken and drowning.

One breath in,
a flood of frustration out—
sweet release.

Another breath—
another glimpse at the big picture.
That tiny human—
that three-foot-tall storm of emotion and energy—
is counting on me.

One more breath
and I fix my face,
pull myself together,
and give motherhood another shot.

My daughter doesn't know Mommy's breaking down
and I'll never tell.

43613

Sunrise on hardworking neighbors—
these sweltering streets
pave a way for our future.
Hope
in our backyard.

You'll grow up together—
trikes to bikes,
adventures with the girl next door.
Friends
rule the neighborhood.

Dark Clouds Over Toledo

The topic of conversation
most days.
The forecast throws us a lifeline.
We feel the extremes
but still make it through.
Low rumbles in the distance
soon leave us drenched and cold.
Our wind-swept brains
are exhausted.
We retreat indoors
and wait for a peek of the sun.

Weekend Aftermath

Giggles in the aftermath of two days off,
messy curls that plot against you,
mischief is barely three feet tall.

Muddy puddles taunt her
with promises of grit and glory.
She stomps with a twinkle in her eye

A concert for those in the grocery store—
she sings the highest of highs.
A hasty scolding is served with a chuckle.

Freshly colored-on walls
and a hyper-vigilant family cat
praise the close of the weekend.

A Little Cheer with Our Cheerios

Tuesday night grocery shopping—
my husband looks
but I noticed her, too.
Crooked smile as she chats on her phone,
raven locks in a loose ponytail,
and black leggings for errand-running
that grab our attention.
We both admire her soft curves.
Thank you to the unknowing siren
for making the cereal aisle more beautiful.

Anxiety

Anxiety is an acid
that eats away
at your thick outer shell,
exposing your insides.
Your brain runs in overdrive
repairing the damage
while still trying to function.
It can't keep up.

I can't keep up.

The Things We Love

Becoming a mom
never meant giving up the things I love.
My daughter needs to see me
doing the things that make me happy
because one day,
I want her to know she can do the same.

As a woman,
your identity is not limited to wife and mom.
You're an individual, too.

Your identity can be
whatever you want it to be.
You don't have to have kids.
You don't have to get married.
But if you do,
let it be something you truly want.

No matter what path you choose,
you're still a strong woman
with passions and goals.
Do what makes you happy
and don't let anyone stand in your way.

Alphabet Soup

My baby won't eat her bowl full of alphabet soup.
She just licks the chocolate spoon before it melts into
    her veins.
She burps soda bubbles—one, two, three of them
that float high to the candy apple sunset.
Her sticky hands cling to her curls.
I whisper, "The letters will free you."
An "F" for her tiny fingers that will pluck dreams from
    the clouds,
an "R" for the reality she will untwist to illuminate her
    future,
and finally, two "E"s for her endless energy.
Her hands loosen and lift her bowl to her face.
She swallows that freedom in one big gulp.

Family Image

A pristine image of a Midwest family—
flawless yet brittle.

They watch football together,
excuse themselves from the table when they're done
    eating,
go to church on Sunday,
and use words like "darn" and "heck."
My four-year-old innocently blurts out four-letter
    words
and her shit-eating grin is the kind of deviance I adore.
I claim responsibility for that.

Why do parents paint this pretty picture —
sweet perfect kids,
a life without challenges,
or natural bodily processes.

I present my daughter with a transparent reality
because the truth is easier to keep up with.
Her childhood is free of fear and dogma
which will hopefully lead to a lifetime free of guilt and
    shame.

Families in the heartland present a polished outer shell
and never talk about anything beneath it.
Fearing god keeps their kids in line—
or so they think.

over →

Ignoring the struggles of your wayward children
won't make their problems go away.
Family secrets can poison overconfident futures.

Don't hold children to expectations you don't hold
    yourself to.
Fuck the image and meet them down on the ground.

For the love of all that's good and pure,
let children be people, too.
They don't need to be hidden or shielded from
    reality—
or ashamed of their own reality.
Let them be real. Let them know real.

Twinkle

Call your child down from the sky—
she's playing with the stars.
She hangs from the crescent moon
and gently blankets the earth in fog.
Descending, swaying
she returns to the ground
in a night owl's feather
then looks up at you.
The stars have gathered in her eyes.
Never extinguish that brilliant twinkle —
don't let it fade with time.
That twinkle will open doors,
open hearts, open minds.

Sleep Lightly

Fading fast
and she insistently wants to play.
My limbs are heavy,
eyelids hard to keep open,
but she begs for more attention.

I need a nap
but feel guilty for taking one.

Sleep is always light
when you have a 24/7 responsibility
that calls you, "mom."

She Came in a Storm

Champagne giggles,
pushing bronze—
we welcomed her
in lightning and wind.
Her future lies
under the turbulent sky.

Memories of tears, sweat, and sleepless nights
fade into adventure.
Seeing her learn about the world
is both heartwarming and heartbreaking.

Each day brings something new—
a new word
a new song
a new lesson
a new fear.

Our mission isn't always clear
but she survived another day
(and so did we).

Just when we feel like giving up,
her toothy smile
and granite eyes squinting in laughter
motivate our purpose once again.

Non-traditional Student

Community college—
where like-minded adults
rush to class after work
and hope for a chance at the ladder.
Climbing higher
with families
jobs
and sometimes second chances.
Diversity,
practicality,
and sacrifice—
key ingredients
in gaining real-world knowledge.
My daughter was nothing but a twinkle in my eye
but I still wanted to make her proud.
Thank you for giving me skills
that I still use today.

Dance for Strangers

Dancing
to her own music
in the middle of the freezer aisle—
her curls
hide the secret to happiness.
Strangers' warm smiles
connect us
to a kinder humanity.
Walls come down
in the neighborhood grocery store.

Why Aren't There More Bright Stars?

I never step out the door
without lipstick,
medium hold curls,
and stomach-turning doubts.
My smile comes with a price,
but my frazzled nerves are free.
There's room for you in my mind
but not my planner.
Your rejection won't sting
if I reject you first.
I don't fit into your little red box.
I bust down the plastic walls
then reapply my lipstick—
Revlon Stellar Sunrise.
You'll turn your back
but still hear me sing.
People are usually disappointing
but I've learned
a few bright stars are worth it.

Part IV

Midwest Mom
Meatloaf and Revolution

The fire inside me

burning my belly,
warming my spine,
fueling my stride,
that stokes my dreams,
drives my vision,
and propels me forward,

shall never be extinguished.

In the Quiet of the Snow

In the quiet of the snow
tears are stiff and frozen
no longer bleeding down her face.

In the quiet of the snow
her painful secrets now exposed
and the conditions of your love revealed.

In the quiet of the snow
you left her all alone
the heavy flakes now resting on her shoulders.

In the quiet of the snow
your tiny world caves in
weighed down by fairytales and shame.

In the quiet of the snow
her passion stokes the fire
illuminating the revolution within our reach.

In the quiet of the snow
she learns to stand on her own.
A world of warmth and love awaits her.

A New War

No options in my fragile reality—
My world unravels or I die in the machine.
One fading chance for a stable future;
I jump headfirst into a shot at equality.

Rusty expectations keep society docile.
Our quiet obedience and hard work
keep our chains in place.
It's time to break the silence and give a damn.

Exhaustion will fire the first bullet—
one last push for us all.
In a cold world made for just a few fat cats,
the workers will rise.

My fingertips are tattered
from the artillery of a new war.
Secrets don't exist on this side of the screen;
the chance at tomorrow is fleeting.

End-stage capitalism is laid to rest
in the confines of my mind.
I'll jump on the bandwagon of desperation
because it takes a village to dig out of this hole.

Lead Like a Girl

Giggles, hair bows, and endless potential—
the future comes home swaddled in pink.
My daughter can save our world.
Call the shots with compassion.
Curious little girls grow up
to be women who lead the way.

Jump

I'm churning through life
recklessly powered by my scorching sincerity.

Dip a toe in the refreshing unknown—
jump without a life jacket.

Nerves beckon my lunch,
tears clear the way.

The only way forward
is by risking it all.

One More

Take it all off,
dive into uncertainty
where my toes don't touch the bottom—
one more splash of cool confidence.

Stars laced with freezer burn
guide my numb extremities
overflowing with hope—
one more slip with fate.

Rolling sweat beads
stoke my passion's fire.
Another day at the grind—
one more glimpse of glory

Taste my bounty
in the wake of goodness.
You lick my spoon bare—
one more pinch of wisdom.

My future footsteps
are in a vulnerable state.
My destiny newly recovered—
one more notch on the dial.

One more look
One more doubt
One more push
One more bite

One more forgiving chance.

I Cleaned My Plate

My curves tell a story
of delicious redemption.

One fateful day this defeated college dropout—
out of exhaustion and desperation—
decided there was nowhere to go but up.
I surrendered to treatment.
With a white flag I reclaimed my life.
What seemed like years of loss,
propelled me into an adulthood of opportunity.

Fabulously fat—
I now love what I once feared
in the insecurities of my youth.
My ass doesn't quit and I really love pizza—
two very liberating revelations
that saved my crumbling confidence.
Stretch marks are battle scars
of bringing a little girl into this world.
Years of a dangerous struggle with an eating disorder
took me to places I never want my daughter to go
and I plan on telling her all about it.
The victory of recovery goes to the whole family.

Fuck society's picture-perfect expectations—
I'll take that last piece of cheesecake
because I'm five feet of living in the moment,
uninhibited smiles,
and big love.

We are all unique works of nature.
Let's embrace our differences
and make this world less boring—

and more beautiful.

Megan Rahn

More of Us

Bottom out—
here and now.
Desperation motivates,
crisis brings change.

Riches of your wildest dreams
reserved for the few
riding on the backs of us all—
I just want to get by:

A stocked pantry.
A car full of gas.
Paying bills with one job.
Time for my daughter.

There are more of us
than there are of them.
We can level the playing field
and guarantee survival for us all.

Fists to the sky,
headlights to the future.
The shackled masses are freed
and leave the shadows behind.

For all the angry mothers
and other workers of the world,
our voices can become one—
a prosperous future within our grasp.

Hungry for food,
starving for change.
The downtrodden people will
claim tomorrow.

We'll Keep You Well

We are all connected
one brain to another
and most of ours are broken.

Our solutions are easy
or complicated
but our wellness is a delicate state.

Stability often comes from a pill bottle
and that's okay—
balance is the hard part.

Be your own normal
in an unforgiving world
of rigid expectations.

Come out of the dark
and brush your tired smile—
we're here to lift you up.

Crawl if you can't walk
but keep moving forward.
Your day in the sun is coming.

Anger

Red
Warm flesh
Heavy forehead
A stomach that stays in my throat
A heart and brain that are bound

Mistreatment
Injustice
A world that is constrained to right now
A voice that needs to be heard—

Silenced.

Combustible.

Our Rope

Tired feet—
a testament to our honest ambitions.

We walk the same street
trying to live above water.

Fingers clinging to sky,
only bubbles acknowledge our fragile existence.

Throw me a rope,
and I'll throw you one, too.

Only rain
trickles down from the top.

But you and I—
we can make the sun shine.

Rise

Appropriate unforgiving anger
and generations of exhaustion
brought us to this inevitable place.

Our broken smiles
and tired brains
show the painful wear of our work.

Income inequality
comes with a terrible price
that the wealthy don't have to pay.

Sparkling promises
undoubtedly fall through
or never come at all.

We're inching closer every day
to victoriously invading
their comfortable position.

To the threatened ballot box,
to the turmoil of our run-down streets—
it's one step at a time in our revolution.

We rise ten feet tall—
standing next to our neighbors,
standing up for a struggling humanity.

We rise
because we have nothing left to lose
and a life worth living to gain.

Free to Roam

Let questions swirl in my brain
as my eyes strain at the glow of the screen.

I'm a tired mom from the heartland
with the world at my fingertips.

Opportunities and choices are overwhelming
in a world becoming so small.

My corner of the planet is now yours
as I peer into your faraway life.

Once impossible connections are made
as I share my story with the world

isolated but no longer alone.

A Mom with Dreams

These wind-swept streets
of pewter and paradise
no longer define
the boundaries of my future.

My dreams may be fading in the twilight
but they have not yet met their demise.
A denim and lava exterior
hides the blue compassion on the inside.

A forward-reaching smile
illuminates my distant memories.
Determination is the ink
scratching off the endless tasks on the board.

Sneakers with holes
tell a sad, tired story
they don't want to hear.
Let the tied-tight laces do the talking.

Outer space ambition faces rusty function.
Firebrick steaming ahead,
charred earth beneath my aching feet—
this mama has glossy expectations.

Keep it moving and conquer doubts.
I'll leave my mark
on this insignificant moment
in a universe that swallows us whole.

The Path

Swim in a sea of goosebumps
and opportunity
because you set the path on fire.
No one is looking
because they're glued to the mirror
counting flaws that don't exist.
But you know true beauty—
purpose grounded in your earthly existence.
Throw away the Book
and make your own way.
Destructive humans on a rotting planet
can show promise
if you let them connect.
Compassion grows
from the heaviest tears.
Change lies under our aching feet.

Girl Mom

How do I protect my daughter
from having the stories all women have,
from fearing the night
and walking alone?

How do I protect my daughter
when rapists run for president,
when boys will be boys,
when an accusation is too frequently overlooked?

How do I protect my daughter
when she doesn't have a say
when her body is property
and legislation dictates her future?

How do I protect my daughter
from seventy-eight cents to the dollar
from taxes that come in pink
from old and rotten expectations?

How do I protect my daughter
from the shards of glass
when she destroys the glass ceiling
and leads the way in a man's world?

How do I support my daughter
when she no longer needs my protection?

Grit

Sweating bullets,
sweating time,
sweating grit between my tired eyes.

A smirk for the ages
has nestled in my luminous stench.

Take a picture to remember
and cross it off the to-do list.

Elbow grease,
sleepless nights—
one step forward in this momma's life.

Many of these poems were written during Ohio's stay-at-home order, a response to the Covid-19 pandemic in the spring of 2020. My daughter and I were home together for three months. I enjoyed the time we had just her and me, and I took advantage of every opportunity I had to write. It was a period of growth for me both as a mom and a writer.

The Virus (Quarantine Poetry)

My tired brain smothered
by a long and winding list of precautions.
Stare at the endless walls
until we call it safe.

One day we'll step out the door
and put our arms
around each other
but not anytime soon.

Empty store shelves,
empty calendars,
empty feeling
in my calloused gut.

Six feet to sanity—
masks and gloves
that collect in the trash
comfort our fear.

Sanitize my driving forces.
I'm one woman alone
on a welcoming portal
connected to the world.

The clock ticks on.
The moon rises behind clouds.
Darkness blankets the city once more
but the sun will rise again.

A virus invades
the bodies and minds
of this aching planet
but solidarity is contagious.

One humanity
against the sickness—
one fierce and hopeful fight
will save us all.

We're in this together.

About the Author

Megan Rahm is a restless mom from Toledo, Ohio who has found her voice in art and writing. Her spirited four-year-old daughter often inspires her work and she never leaves her house without her Chromebook and Sharpies. She loves Toledo's weather and hates Costco on a Saturday afternoon. Being an atheist plays a significant role in her life. She never thought she could be open about it, but this book is her coming-out party and everyone's invited.

CPSIA information can be obtained
at www.ICGtesting.com
Printed in the USA
LVHW020439040523
745965LV00007B/357

9 780988 493889